Launch Legally: Business Plan Workbook

A Guide for Entrepreneurs Who Are Ready To Get Ish Done

Launch Legally: Business Plan Workbook, A Guide for Entrepreneurs Who Are Ready To Get Ish Done

TABLE OF CONTENTS

TABLE OF CONTENTS

Introduction

A Business Plan, Really?

Launching a successful business requires clarity, hard work and dedication. There will be many late nights and early mornings. Are you ready?

What is clarity?

Clarity is having clearness or understanding. It is being free from indistinctness or ambiguity. Clarity is essential to succeeding in both life and business. Being clear on what is important to succeed in life allows you to navigate through life like Neo from the Matrix, dodging obstacles that distract you from your path. This allows you to focus on your goals and pursue them fervently.

Gaining clarity over your life requires being brutally honest about your ambitions. Next determine what steps you need to take to make your ambitions a reality. Finally become diligent in only accepting opportunities that further your goals.

Purchasing this workbook means one of your goals is to become a business owner. Clarity in business is especially important as one can quickly become overwhelmed by the amount of work it takes to be successful. I find that much of success comes from having a clear understanding of what the business does, who are your customers and why you are going into business? The best way to gain clarity in business is to create a business plan.

So What Exactly Is A Business Plan Exactly?

Many business owners know they need a business plan but are hindered by uncertainty. Some skip this step and try diving right into the money. These entrepreneurs fail to realize business plans provide clarity for their business allowing them to operate without chaos or confusion. Writing a business plan makes you analyze from the beginning whether there is a market for your business and where you fit in that market. Some may think clarity in business is overrated however, potential investors and banks are more likely to invest and provide financing to businesses that can show exactly how much it will cost to start their business, how long it will take the business to make money and how long it will take the business to make a profit.

What Should My Business Plan Include?

Business Plans have several components contained in the 6 main categories. Those categories are as follows:

1. The Executive Summary

The executive summary is the most important part of your business plan especially if you are seeking outside funding. It is the first contact that potential investors have with your business, other than yourself. Contrary to what the name suggest, this section is not a summary of your business plan but rather to cause the reader to act. It allows the reader to know within a matter of minutes whether they should give you, the business owner, the time of day. The purpose of the executive summary is to entice the reader to read your business plan or even better, to meet with you to discuss your business. Most investors won't take the time to read your business plan from beginning to end unless they have a compelling reason to. So it is your responsibility to do just that.

The executive summary as with the rest of the business plan must be written with the reader in mind. It should be well written, factual and easy to read.

2. Company Profile

The company profile provides the reader with more detail of who your company is. It will discuss the founders, your business structure and your product/service. Completing this section gives you the opportunity to seriously consider what motivated you to start the business in the first place, where you see your company in the future and what values your company stand for. The reader will learn about your experience in the industry in addition to the company's short term and long - term goals. Most importantly the reader will gain in depth knowledge about your product/service. They will learn what the product or service is, what it does and who it was designed to benefit.

3. Marketing Plan

The marketing plan describes exactly how you intend to communicate with the market and articulates how you want consumers to connect with you. In this section you will identify your target market and ideal client. That is the consumers who will find the most value from your product or service and out of those consumers the ones who you would most like to work with. Identifying your market helps you know how to speak to your client's pain points in such a way that you are never selling but rather providing a solution to a problem they are having. You should spend a considerable amount of time on this section because it doesn't matter how wonderful your product or service is if no one knows about it.

4. Management Profile

If you are a new company this section may be relatively short, as you may be the only person making decisions. The management profile section will discuss the company's founders, their experience in the industry, any relevant accomplishments, their education and role in the company. You will include this same information for other senior team members, board of directors, board of advisors and any consultant that assist the company in making major decisions.

5. Operational Plan

The operational plan concerns how your business will bring its product or service to market. It discusses where your raw material will come from. Raw materials refer to the basic material that the product is made from. This section also discusses what employees or contractors you need to create your product or facilitate service, what qualifications they will have and whether there is a sizable pool of talent to choose from. It is important to discuss the facility you will operate out of, including square footage and price. Additionally, this section needs to provide detail information on all major equipment that is required to produce your product or service.

6. Financial Plan

The financial section of your business plan is a combination of actual and forecast information. Although most people won't bother to read your entire business plan, most will take a quick peak at the numbers located in this section. Your income statement, balance sheet and cash flow statement give a quick view of your company's current value, your ability to pay the bills, and make a profit. In a nutshell this section will immediately inform you and the reader whether you have a viable business or if you are wasting your time and money.

How To Use This Workbook

Launch Legally: The Business Plan Workbook, was created to assist new and existing business in developing a strong foundation for their business. A strong foundation requires the ability to communicate essential information about your business such as what your business does, who it does it for, why it does it and whether or not you're making any money doing it. This workbook asks you questions designed to pull out intimate details of your business. It will take time and effort to complete this workbook as you do keep the following in mind:

- The information contained within the workbook is not a substitute for legal advice.
- Take time to answer each question thoroughly
- Realize that some questions will require outside research
- Know that all of the information is not necessary for your business plan to investors and other third parties, but all of the information is necessary to you as the business owner
- You can complete the workbook alone or
- Schedule a Clarity Session with Attorney LaConya Murray by emailing her office at admin@laconyamurray.com or calling 334-523-0022.

Let's get started.

Personal Goals

Defining your Why

Personal Goals

Defining Your Why

Before you start drafting your business plan let's discuss why you are going into business for yourself in the first place. Articulating your why improves your chances of success in business because it keeps you focused and serves as a reminder during your journey through entrepreneurship.

1. Why are you starting your business

2. What personal goals do you wish to accomplish by starting your own business? (More time with family, travel more, etc…)

3. List your household expenses plus any extracurricular activities.

4. What is your minimum salary you can make to sustain your current standard of living?

Opportunity Awaits

Defining the Problem and Solution

Opportunity Awaits

Defining the Problem and Solutions

Clarity Discussion: Studies show that businesses that are created to fill an opportunity have a greater chance of success than those started out of necessity. Successful business owners see a problem and create a solution to fill it.

I. Problem Solving:

1. What problem are you solving?

2. What is occurring as a result of this problem?

3. When does this problem occur and how often?

4. Who has this problem?

5. What is the source of the problem?

6. Has anyone specifically asked you to solve this problem? If so approximately how many?

Opportunity Awaits

Defining the Problem and Solutions

Clarity Discussion: Opportunities are everywhere but the most lucrative one come straight from the consumer's mouth. What are they constantly asking for? What are the constantly complaining about?

II. Solution Base Business

1. How can this problem be solved?

2. How will the solution be implemented?

3. How does you market want you to solve this problem?

4. What are alternative ways of implementing?

5. Why is your solution the best solution to the problem?

Marketing Plan

Defining Your Market

Marketing Plan

Defining Your Market

I. Industry Information

1. Identify your industry?

2. How many new business were started in the last 5 year to accommodate the problem you identified in section I. (Clarity point: You can use Uncle Google to find this information. Try google.com/trends)

3. Is industry growing, stable, declining? How can you tell?

4. How has technology affected the way the industry does business today compared to 5 years ago?

5. How will it affect the way business is done 3 years from now?

II. Identify Your Target Market

Clarity Discussion: Defining your target market allows you to focus your marketing dollars the specific market that is more likely to buy from you. It is a group of prospects that can be defined by a broad range of possible characters, including but not limited to:

- geographic location,
- lifestyle,
- hobbies,
- income,
- occupation,
- education,
- gender,
- etc…

This is not to be defined by ideal client, which we will define later

6. What geographically area is your target market located?

7. What level of education do they have?

8. Are they married?

9. Do they have any children?

10. What is their income level?

11. Do they work in a particular industry? If yes what industry?

12. What is their age demographic?

After you define your target market answer the following questions

a. Approximately how many people are in your target market?

b. Can they afford your product/service?

Yes ☐ No ☐

c. Are they easily accessible?

Yes ☐ No ☐

d. How will they benefit from your product/service?

III. Identify Your Ideal Client

Clarity Discussion: Your ideal clients are the people in your target market whom you want to work with more than anyone else. They are the ones who possible share your strange sense of humor, they see the value of paying for the type of service you provide, maybe they're tech/computer savvy, they allow you to work and don't bug you unless there is an emergency.

You get the point.

1. What attributes does your ideal client have?

IV. Identify Competitors In Your Market

Clarity Discussion: At this point you need to be able to readily identify any one who provides similar product/service to your target market and ideal client. Remember that competitors are not limited to companies that provide similar product/service.

Direct competitors are businesses that offer the same product/services and serve the same customers as your business.

Indirect competitors, on the other hand, are businesses that may offer the same product or services as your business however, these products or services are not their primary products or services offered

The top 5 competitors in my market are:

1) ________________

a. The average price for the product/service they provide is?

b. How many years have they been in business?

c. How do they compete with your business?

2) ______________

a. The average price for the product/service they provide is?

b. How many years have they been in business?

c. How do they compete with your business?

3) ______________

a. The average price for the product/service they provide is?

b. How many years have they been in business?

c. How do they compete with your business?

4) ________________

a. The average price for the product/service they provide is?

b. How many years have they been in business?

c. How do they compete with your business?

5) ________________

a. The average price for the product/service they provide is?

b. How many years have they been in business?

c. How do they compete with your business?

2. What message do you want your brand to convey?

3. How are you doing that?

4. How will you package your product/service?

5. What promotional items are you using? (cards, brochures, pens, etc…)

6. What do they look like? (describe or attach samples)

VI. How Will You Promote Your Business?

Clarity Discussion: Many people confuse marketing with branding. Branding is the look, feel and consistency of the language your business presents to consumers. (Courtesy of my friend Tani Chambers of tanichambers.com)

Marketing is the art of having your product or service exactly where your client is. This is why it is important to understand your client's pain points and know where they are going for help. A successful business understands the differences between branding and marketing and utilizes both.

1. Identify at least five avenue of marketing that you will use.

- [ ] Word of mouth
- [ ] Door to door
- [ ] Client referrals
- [ ] Direct Mail
- [ ] Indoor advertising
- [ ] Host special event
- [ ] Google Ads
- [ ] Outdoor advertising
- [ ] Print Advertising
- [ ] Point of sale advertising
- [ ] Professional referrals
- [ ] Write for third parties
- [ ] Pubic Relations
- [ ] Radio
- [ ] Workshops
- [ ] Vending
- [ ] Television
- [ ] Email
- [ ] Sponsorships
- [ ] Social Media
  - [ ] Facebook
  - [ ] YouTube
  - [ ] Instagram
  - [ ] Pinterest
  - [ ] LinkedIn
- [ ] Other

Company Profile

Defining Your Business

Company Profile

Defining Your Business

Clarity Discussion: It is amazing (and scary) how many people start businesses but do not know the intimidate details of their business. As a business owner it is your responsibility to know who your business is, what it does, why it does it, and who it does it for. This section is designed to do just that.

I. Who Your Business Is?

1. What is your company's name?

Clarity Discussion: There are several issues to consider when naming your company. Often times your name is a consumer's first introduction to your product or service. What impression do you want to give? Is it relevant to the product or service? Can it be protected? Some say that naming your company after yourself is the way to go, some believe that the best names are informative, while others believe that fanciful made up names leave a lasting impression. Whatever name you choose remember it is in fact your company that makes the name not the other way around.

2. What is your Business Structure? (Are you operating as a sole proprietor, partnership, limited liability company, or corporation). You can refer to the chart on the following page to determine the benefits of each.

	Sole Proprietorship	Partnership	LLC	Corporation (C-Corp)	S-Corp
Definition	One person doing business with absolute control of the business operations	Two or more people come together to do business for profit as co-owners	Provides for limited liability and division of profits among owners	Legal entity that is separate from its owners	Legal entity that is separate from its owners and allows for the company's profits and losses to be passed through to the shareholders
How to Start	Apply for state and/or federal tax numbers	Apply for state and/or federal tax numbers and create an agreement between partners	Apply for appropriate tax numbers, register with proper state agency, choose registered agent to accept service of process	Apply for appropriate tax numbers, prepare and file Articles of Incorporation with proper state agency and Bylaws	Apply for appropriate tax numbers, prepare and file Articles of Incorporation with proper state agency and Bylaws
Taxation	Business's earnings are taxed once and pass through the owner	Business's earnings are taxed once and earnings are divided among partners based on agreement	Earnings are taxed once.	The corporation is taxed based on earnings and then owners are taxed for dividends	Earnings divided among owners and taxed only once
Personal Liability	Owner's liability is unlimited	All partner's liability is unlimited unless otherwise stated in an agreement	Owners maintain control of the business and have limited liability for debts and liabilities of the business	Personal assets are protected. Liability is limited to the corporation's assets	Personal assets are protected. Liability is limited to the corporation's assets
Transfer of Ownership	No	Based on agreement	Yes	Yes	Yes
Control of Day-to-Day Operations	Owner	Based on agreement	Owner	Officers	Board of Directors
Number of Owners	1	2 or more	1 or more	1 or more	No more than 100

3. Where is the business' headquarter located?

4. What inspired the creation of the business?

5. When was the business started?

6. List the company's founder members.

7. What is the trading name of the entity?

ClarityDiscussion: A trade name is the name you a business uses in commerce other than its official business name. This name is protected under trademark law. In addition to registering your trade name as a trademark you need to register it with the appropriate state or county office to avoid being held personally liable for contracts entered into on behalf of the trade name.

8. Describe you business's operations (e.g. days and hours of operations)

9. Briefly describe your business and the product and/or service you provide.

10. Where will your business be located? (Will you have a brick and mortar office, operate strictly online or both? List the address (physical or web)

11. List the contact information for your business such as, websites, email addresses, fax, landline, and mobile numbers.

12. List the contact information of your business advisors (e.g. accountants, lawyers, bankers etc.)

13. Where will your business be located? (Will you have a brick and mortar office, operate strictly online or both? List the address (physical or web)

14. Identify what licenses, permits and regulations will affect your business.

15. If you are looking for a bank loan, a private investment, a partner, etc., what are your reasons for seeking this type of investment? How will this investment benefit this particular partner or investor?

16. If you already have an existing business and are creating your plan in order expand your business, you must provide a history of your business. Provide the following information: The current owner of the business, current location, how many years the business has been in existence, strengths, weaknesses, market share, and financial information for the last three to five years.

Company Profile

Defining Your Business

Clarity Point: It is important to offer services and products at different price points (high, medium, low)

II. What Does Your Business Do?

1. What high end product/service are you offering ?

a. What is the name of your product/service?

b. Describe the product/service?

c. Who would benefit from your product/service? (Clarity Point: You can refer back to the problem section and target market for help)?

d. What is included?

e. How will it be distributed (website, webinar, workshops, one on one, department stores, boutiques, etc)

Company Profile

Defining Your Business

Clarity Point: It is important to offer services and products at different price points (high, medium, low)

II. What Does Your Business Do?

2. What medium end product/service are you offering ?

a. What is the name of your product/service?

b. Describe the product/service?

c. Who would benefit from your product/service? (Clarity Point: You can refer back to the problem section and target market for help)?

d. What is included?

e. How will it be distributed (website, webinar, workshops, one on one, department stores, boutiques, etc)

Company Profile

Defining Your Business

Clarity Point: It is important to offer services and products at different price points (high, medium, low)

II. What Does Your Business Do?

3. What low end product/service are you offering?

a. What is the name of your product/service?

b. Describe the product/service?

c. Who would benefit from your product/service? (Clarity Point: You can refer back to the problem section and target market for help)?

d. What is included?

e. How will it be distributed (website, webinar, workshops, one on one, department stores, boutiques, etc)

4. What future product/services will you provide?
Estimated Launch Date?

Company Profile

Defining Your Business

III. Why Does Your Business Do What It Does?

4. What is your Mission Statement? (The mission statement explains what your company does. It gives your customers and the community an idea what your business is about.)

5. What is your Vision Statement? (The vision statement explains your company's goals. It answers the question of where do you see yourself in the future.)

6. What is your Value Statement? (The value statement informs your customers and those you work with of your core beliefs and top priorities.)

7. What is your Purpose Statement? (The purpose statement states why your company exists in the first place.)

8. Describe the company's short- term goals (1-2 yrs).

9. Describe the company's long- term goals (5-10 yrs).

Team Profile

Defining Your Team

Team Profile

Defining Your Team

I. Who's On Your Team?

Clarity Discussion: When business starts picking up, you may consider hiring additional team members. Before you place your help wanted ads ask yourself these three questions:
1) Is the growth temporary or seasonal;
2) Is my business suffering as the result of the growth; and
3) Do I really need the help?

If your analysis leads you to the conclusion that you are ready to hire help make sure you hire wisely. When interviewing potential candidates ask yourself if the person ha the experience you are looking for, the strengths needed to fulfill the position and will they fit well with the culture of you company.

1. Business owner #1

a. What roles do they currently play?

b. What roles will they play in the future?

2. Business owner #2

a. What roles do they currently play?

b. What roles will they play in the future?

3. Business owner #3

a. What roles do they currently play?

b. What roles will they play in the future?

4. What employees, if any, do you have and what role do they play in the company?

5. What skills and qualification does each person have? (Summarize noteworthy skills and qualification and attach resume)

6. What future team members will you need?

7. What skills and/or qualification will they have? (Describe the skill and qualification for each position)

8. How will they increase revenue? (Explain how each future hire will increase your business revenue qualification for each position)

9. What factors are necessary to determine when it is time to make new?

Financial Profile

Defining Your Numbers

Financial Profile

Defining Your Numbers

I. What Does It Cost To Be The Boss?

Clarity Discussion: The financial section is critical to determine the viability of your business. This is important information for not only investors but for you as the business owner. Wouldn't you love to know if your business makes sense financially BEFORE you poured your tears, blood and sweat into it?

1. List the cost associated with your business. Identify whether it is a reoccurring cost (if so how often) or a start up cost. This includes rent, salaries, insurance, office supplies, advertisement, taxes, deposits, etc...

Expenses Continued....

2. How will you keep up with your records, inventory, sales, money received, etc…

II. Business Assets?

Clarity Discussion: Intellectual property just like real property increases your assets. Identifying your trademarks, copyrights, and patents is a crucial step for your business because it can be sold, licensed or used to negotiate more favorable contracts.

- Trademarks are brand identifier. It is that thing that distinguishes your company from another. This could be your logo, trade name, or a specific color (think Tiffany & Co.).

- Copyrights are used to protect literary works and other works of expression. This work includes poems, songs, plays, music, and computer programs just to name a few.

- A patent is a grant from the U.S. Government to exclude others from making, using, selling, or importing another person's new, non-obvious, and useful invention. The protection is limited to the United States for a term determined by the type of patent the owner receives.

1. Identify any and all trademarks associated with the product/service.

2. Identify any and all copyrights associated with the product/service.

4. Identify any and all patents associated with the product/service.

5. Identify any and all other assets owned by the business

III. Money Goals

At the very beginning of this workbook you calculated your household expenses to determine the minimum amount of income you would need to survive. This exercises assumes that you do not just want to survive you want to live. Keep this exercise in mind as you complete the financial section of the workbook.

1. How much income do you want to earn in 12 months?

a. Divide that amount by 12 to calculate your monthly goal

b. Divide the monthly goal by 52 to calculate your weekly goal

c. Divide the weekly goal by 7 to calculate your daily goal

2. How many products/services do you need to sell/provide to achieve your monetary goals?

a. Yearly

b. Monthly

c. Weekly

d. Daily

IV. Funding Your Business

Clarity Discussion: Start up financing refers to where the money necessary for start up will come from. There are several sources of financing including self-financing, loans, crowd funding, capital ventures, and angel investors. You will find a definition along with a brief pro and con of each below.

Bootstrapping

Clarity Discussion: Bootstrapping is a method in which most first time entrepreneurs do by self-starting a company using his/her
own finances.

Pro: Bootstrapping makes an entrepreneur customer focused which gives them enough room to create a great product and gain loyal customers.

Con: Time constraints. When one is bootstrapping their business, chances are they are juggling a day job while running the business at the same time.

1. What will each of the founding members contribute?

a. Founder's Name and how much

b. Founder's Name and how much

c. Founder's Name and how much

d. Founder's Name and how much

Loans/Lines of Credit

Clarity Discussion: Lines of credit refers to several options or types of borrowing money that is usually pre-approved from a bank, a pawnshop, a social lending institution, a payday lender and even from friends or family.

Pro: Low interest rates and offers a more flexible repayment schedule.

Con: A borrower undergoes a credit evaluation process to determine his or her credit history and depending on the bank or financial institution's assessment, one will either be approved or disapproved.

2. Will there be any loans or lines of credit?

Yes No

a. If yes, where/who will the loan/credit come from? (Family, friends, bank, home equity, etc…)

b. How much is the loan for?

c. What are the repayment terms?

c. What are the repayment terms?

Crowd Funding

Clarity Discussion: Crowd funding is the method of
raising money to finance a new business or a project by means of seeking donations from other people using a certain platform - usually through the Internet.

Pro: It does not
require any upfront fees and it is a great way to raise money quickly, get business feedback and attract investors to your product or idea.

Con: It puts your business idea at risk since anybody can learn about it and actually steal the concept and copy it

3. Will you raise money through crowd funding?

Yes No

a. What platform will you use?

b. Why did you choose this platform?

c. What are the benefits of using this platform?

d. What are the consequences of using this platform?

Venture Capital

Clarity Discussion: Venture Capital is a non-traditional financing source that typically exchanges cash in exchange for shares and active role in the business. (Think Shark Tank)

Pro: Perfect for startups who need a bigger capital plus consulting or help guide in their business.

Con: Expects about 50 percent in rate of return.

1. Will you receive money through venture capitalist?

Yes No

a. If yes, what VC?

b. How money did you receive?

c. What are the terms of the agreement? (Summarize the terms and attach the written terms of the agreement)

Angel Investors

Clarity Discussion: An Angel Investor refers to anybody who is willing to invest money by lending capital to startups or entrepreneurs. This could be anybody among friends and family.

Pro: Investing is based on trust to the borrower and is focused on helping the startup grow.

Con: Seeks a higher rate of return - usually at 25 percent.

1. Will you receive money through Angel Investors?

Yes

No

a. If yes, who are they?

b. How money did you receive?

c. What are the terms of the agreement? (Summarize the terms and attach the written terms of the agreement)

Executive Summary

Summarizing It All

Putting It All Together

Clarity Discussion: Although the executive summary is the first section of the business plan it is the last section of the workbook because it is a summary of all of the information you gathered above. The name is a bit misleading because although it is called a summary the purpose of this section is to recommend a decision. Your executive summary should include the following information:

- The problem
- The solution
- Risk involved
- How you will overcome risk
- Why now is the time to act
- What you need to provide your solution (the investment)

The executive summary like your entire business plan should be realistic, concise and factual. An excellent example of how to write your executive summary can be found here.

Write your own executive summary

Conclusion

Wrapping It Up

Congratulations! You pushed through, asked the tough questions and completed this workbook. Now quick, press save AND print a copy to store in a safe place. You will refer to this information time and time again. Pull it out when you feel like giving up you will use this book to remind yourself why you started your business in the first place. It will either motivate you to keep pushing or you will learn that your "why" is no longer relevant and that it is time to reevaluate. Refer to the book at least quarterly to ensure that you making decisions that further your business' purpose and mission.

Finally, reference it to hold yourself accountable for the goals you set for your business.

Just as it is important to enter your business with a clear plan in mind it is just as important to make sure that you update your plan as need. Over time the market will change and you will
to adjust with it. You will accomplish goals that you set for yourself and need to set new goals. You will grow, add new products/services and your business plan will need to change accordingly.

About The Author

Known as The Brand Attorney, LaConya Murray is the founder and owner of Off the Mark Ip Solutions, a boutique legal and business consulting firm based in Montgomery, Al. Attorney Murray provides legal solutions in the fields of trademarks, copyrights and contracts.

In addition, Ms. Murray offers strategic business consulting sessions for new and existing businesses to assist them with defining their market and identifying revenue streams for their business.

Ms. Murray is also the author of the, "Launch Legally: The Legal Basics Handbook"

To learn more about her services visit www.laconyamurray.com or call 334-523-0022.

Made in United States
North Haven, CT
04 November 2026

21734475R00064